Designed by Artes Graphicae Ltd. Compiled by Zita Alden.
Copyright © MCMLXXIV by Osbro Productions, Inc.
All rights reserved throughout the world.
Published in Great Britain by World Distributors (Manchester) Limited.
P.O. Box 111, 12 Lever Street, Manchester M60 1TS.
Printed in Great Britain by Jarrold & Sons Ltd., Norwich.
SBN 7235 0285 4

OSMONDS
ANNUAL 1975

A big Hello from Mrs Osmond	6
Big Brother is watching you	8
I don't believe in secrets	12
Let me in	16
Fan Club	25
Donny	26
The Osmonds at home	30
Discography	33
The Osmond Foundation	34
Marie, the other Osmond	36
QUIZ	38
Jay the joker of the pack	49
What do you know?	53
Date with a dreamboat	54
How not to drop a clanger on a date	56
You too can look great	58
If the Osmonds drop by . . .	62
Jimmy	64
The Osmond People	68
Up, Up and Away	70
Marie's Mart	72
Goin' Home	76
ANSWERS	77

HIGH THERE!

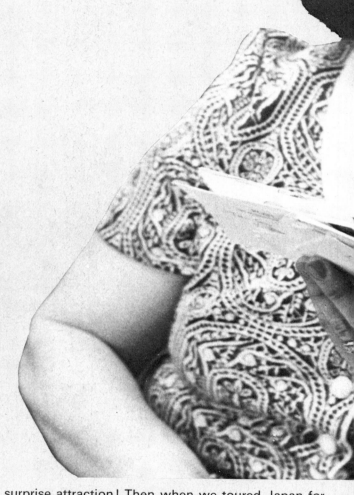

Well, it's twelve years now since the boys first appeared on the Andy Williams TV show and got the break they had all been hoping for. What a hectic and happy time it's been since then.

Andy and his TV audience liked them so much that he signed the boys — there were only four of them, then — for a five-year contract. How about that for a show of confidence. We have a lot to thank Andy for. You know, the boys grew to love Andy during the time they spent on his show.

Alan was only fourteen then, and Jay, who was the youngest singing Osmond at that time, was only eight years old.

Originally we came out West with the idea of staying for a two week holiday, and we ended up buying a new home there. We still kept the ranch in Utah though, because all our memories and closest friends and relations were there. The boys were a bit upset at the thought of having to leave their grandparents, too. So Father and I weren't keen to give up the old home.

My, oh my! Those years certainly were very busy. First of all the boys were having to go to school, just like other children, and they had just as much home-work as the others in spite of the fact that they were now really in show business. Fancy going to work and to school, all at the same time. They rehearsed every time they had a spare moment at home with Father, although the actual recordings usually took part of only one evening each week. I still made sure that they all kept to their regular bed-times, though, because I do feel that, as the old saying goes: "early to bed, early to rise, makes a man healthy, wealthy and wise". It certainly does seem to make them healthy, for without good, strong health they couldn't possibly hope to do the fantastic amount of working and travelling that they do.

We didn't want the boys to miss out on all the things that other children did, so we tried to squeeze as much into each day as we possibly could. We even made room for dancing lessons. Alan and Wayne had taken a few lessons back home in Utah, but they were just the sort of dance steps that most children learn as they go along. Merrill and Jay had been too young to have any real lessons in dancing, although they had picked up bits and pieces here and there by copying the older boys. While they were working on the Andy Williams show, choreographer Jack Rigas became more and more interested in them, and took them under his wing.

Well, as you know, they've come a long way since then. Merrill is now married to a really lovely girl, Mary, and we're delighted to make her one of our big happy family.

The boys are all much older and more experienced, and of course, Donny and Jimmy became part of the group. And Marie is doing well.

Jimmy joined the older boys at the ripe old age of three — while we were doing a tour of Sweden — as a surprise attraction! Then when we toured Japan for the second time in 1969, Jimmy already had a number two hit in Japanese!

Donny also began to hit the headlines in 1969 — so that really was a hectic and busy year for all of us. At about this time the boys began to get sacks and sacks of fan mail. Donny, for instance, a comparative 'new boy', was already getting over 5,000 letters each and every week.

They did their own TV spectacular in 1970 — all on their own. My, weren't we all nervous! But I am happy to say that we all put a terrific amount of hard work into that show, and it was a success; in fact it got very high ratings, and out of more than 500 shows produced each month in the States we were third!

We had our first American concert tour in 1971, and played about fifty cities. Boy, that tired us all out, so that we all went to our ranch in Utah for a well

deserved rest. This was the time when Donny began to make solo recordings, although he was still a very important member of the whole group.

In 1972 we began to become well-known in Britain, and that gave us all great pleasure. Especially when in May that year the boys were invited to perform for the Queen.

We visited Britain again in November for a tour, and again, very briefly, in late 1973. About that 1973 tour. The boys were all excited and delighted to be back in England and the only thing that spoiled it was the sad mishap at Heathrow Airport when some of our fans were injured by the collapse of part of the airport wall. We were all very upset that this should have happened, and were very grateful that the accident wasn't worse.

In late 1973, too, Marie made her hit record, *Paper Roses*. So that by the time we returned for another British tour in 1974, the group had grown even bigger!

Who knows what will happen in 1975? Any guesses?

Thank you for being such fantastic people — we hope that we will be able to spend a little more time in your country next year, and get to know some more of you better.

Bye for now,

Best wishes, and good reading . . .

Mother

BIG BROTH WATCHING

If you're the eldest in your family, do you ever get fed up with being made responsible for your younger brothers and sisters? Well, Alan, the oldest singing Osmond, has the responsibility of looking after his brothers and sister. He's the eldest in the group, and therefore he's the one, next to Mother and Father, who has to act as guardian and protector, mother and father figure; he's the one the others confide their problems, troubles and secrets to.

He's the person who's sometimes perhaps overlooked by lots of the fans who devote their time and energy to the younger brothers.

But Alan's not complaining about his extra responsibility, which comes on top of being lead guitar in the group. Although Mother and Father Osmond always come with the boys on tour, there is such a lot to do at these times that Alan is conscripted to help, and his job is to see that his younger brothers don't get into too many scrapes, or that they don't get too tired.

Being a superstar has its problems as well as its pleasures. There is nothing the boys like better than meeting up with their fans, for they all know it is the fans who have helped so much to make them what they are. But brother Alan keeps an eye on the boys, to make sure they don't get too enthusiastic. He says: "It's hard to tell my brothers that they are getting too tired to go on. You see, if they just spent all their

R IS
YOU

time meeting their fans, they'd have no time left to do their show, let alone all the rehearsals, recording sessions and reading their fan mail. It's not easy, but it's necessary. After all, the family is the thing: someone's got to do the difficult jobs.

The younger brothers are so much in demand – not just from you, the fans, but from people like photographers and newspaper reporters, and they don't like to have to say no. That's where the helping hand, or voice, of big brother comes in – Alan says no for them. Otherwise they'd be up all night, and just think how exhausted they'd become.

When things go wrong, Alan talks them out of the doldrums. And to boost morale when someone's down in the dumps you've really got to forget all your own problems and just concentrate on cheering them up. This can be hard at times, especially if you are not feeling too great your-

self. Alan has a full time job, when he's not playing his lead guitar with the act, keeping his eyes and ears open for any problems that might crop up.

Sometimes the pace gets a bit too hot, and they all run the risk of overtiring themselves – that's when Alan steps in. He doesn't hover over the boys like a horrible school prefect or wicked stepmother or something. He's very proud of them all, and loves being part of a big, happy family. He actually likes being the eldest of the bunch. All the brothers come to him with all their odds and ends. They talk about important things sometimes. But Alan likes to feel that they want to come to him with any problem, however small or petty it may seem. You know yourself how easy it is to discuss big things with people, but it's much more difficult to talk about the little things, because we think people have

too many problems of their own which may be more important to them. Or maybe we think they're going to laugh at us. But you know the old saying about a "trouble shared is a trouble halved". That's true. It does you good to get little problems off your chest – that way they stand less chance of turning into big fat hairy nightmare ones!

I wonder when Alan finds the time to do anything else. But he's full of energy – it must be all that peanut butter and healthy orange juice he consumes. Because in between recording sessions, photo calls, interviews, dealing with fan letters, rehearsing, performing live shows and keeping a brotherly eye on the others, he writes songs, helps in the actual production of their records, and is also a very keen photographer.

And if he feels like a change, his great 'getaway' thing is to go somewhere quiet and listen to music.

Merrill married Mary Carlsen on 17th September 1973, in Salt Lake City Mormon Temple. He knew that it might upset many of his fans the whole world over, but hoped that they would all understand.

"I was first introduced to Mary on a blind date with Alan, and from the first second I saw her it was love at first sight."

She was everything that Merrill had ever dreamed of. He was aware of her beautiful smile which lit up her whole face, and her shining personality, right from the beginning. Mary is the sort of person who makes all the people she comes in contact with happy, because she is a very content and sincere person. She has the gift of making you feel wanted and happy – and that's one of the best feelings to experience.

Merrill and Mary had a whirlwind romance, because they met each other in June, and married in September the same year. In between came their summer tour, which meant there was a great gap, when they didn't even see each other. Their first proper date after their initial meeting was at Robert Redford's 'Sundance'. Mary was twenty-two

when they married, just two years older than Merrill, and had planned to become a schoolteacher. In fact, she hadn't been teaching long before Merrill whisked her away from American Fork High School. Now she teaches only Marie and Jimmy.

As soon as Merrill asked Mary to marry him, when he returned from their August '73 tour, the news was announced to the world's press and the fan clubs.

"I don't believe that my fans will stop liking me just because I've married," he says. "That's why I didn't try to keep my romance a secret. Anyway, you don't keep secrets from those whom you love, and who love you. And I love my fans and would like them to continue to love me, too. There are many different kinds of love, as we all know, and I am sure that my fans will understand about Mary and me, and the way in which we love each other. We all have a great capacity for loving, in many different kinds of ways."

Although the wedding attracted a tremendous amount of interest, the family felt it was really a very private occasion, and tried to keep it among the closest family circle.

ecrets says, Merrill

Mary's wedding dress was a dream. At the front it was floor length, and at the back it got longer and became a train. At the bottom there was a six-inch ruffle. The top was made entirely of lace, decorated with a white satin ribbon. The waist was high; there were long sleeves and another ruffle right around the wrist. The skirt was composed of layers and layers of material, the top one being a kind of chiffon – all soft and flowing.

There were so many people around when Merrill and Mary married that they had to get to the church via an underground tunnel. Only the older members of the family were actually present at the wedding ceremony since you have to have 'gone through the temple' before you are allowed into the inner parts of the building where the wedding took place. There was a wedding breakfast afterwards for 200 friends and relations, followed by a reception in Los Angeles, given by Mike Curb and Ed Leffler. Also a party for over 1,200 friends later the following month in Heber, Utah.

Did you know that Mormon bridegrooms wear a special white robe to be married in? Merrill did, too, although he appears in the photos

13

afterwards in a navy pin-striped suit. There were no bridesmaids, no best man, and according to Mormon tradition, no flowers at the wedding.

Mary and Merrill began their married life together in a house next door to brother Virl, and spend as much time as they can together in it, making it into the perfect first home.

Merrill's biggest fan . . .
Would you believe that Mary had never seen her husband on stage until after they were married! She said afterwards "It felt strange to see Merrill on stage – but it was terrific, and I'm now one of his greatest fans!"

What the others say . . .
Merrill is one of the most fantastically funny guys around. It's not that he tells jokes all over the place, because he certainly doesn't do that – we leave all the funny stuff to Jay! It's just that his actions are all so funny. For example, Merrill has a habit of going mad during recording sessions. Right in the middle of a recording session he suddenly starts singing like a baby. You know, he's learned the way an infant speaks, and he's caught the right voice and vocabulary from the Osmond nephews. You should just hear it. The boys all roll about in stitches and the recording session comes to a grinding halt. They just can't stop, and nearly laugh themselves silly.

One of the family nicknames for him is 'Bear'. You might think that this is a daft name for him, but you see, when Jimmy was very, very young, he thought that the family were all calling his big brother 'bear'. What they were actually saying was 'Merr', for short.

Another of Merrill's nicknames is 'Mr Big-time'. Merrill always had great plans for himself, so Mr Big-time was a name that the family thought suited him.

Mr Big-time is very talented. He always comes up with great ideas for the act, and they are mostly used. One of his fantastic ideas was to put the smoke routine into the act for

Crazy Horses on stage. The boys thought that it would be impossible at first when he mentioned it. But Mother and Father always taught them to think that 'impossible' was a word with which you shouldn't be associated. Donny thought the idea was great, and worked on it like mad to get it into the act.

Merrill is also a very talented choreographer, and a fantastic dancer. He thinks up most of the dance routines, and he picks up things very quickly.

He really is very versatile. He helps Lee, the designer, to plan the clothes specially made for the boys on stage. He loves the colours brown and lavender. Often lavender is worked on to their stage costumes – that's Merrill's influence at work.

When he's not painting and doing things to his new house, he takes out his Nikon camera and takes pictures of the family. It's a hobby which most of the family shares. He writes poetry and songs, too. In fact, I don't know what the group would do without him. He has actually written a few of the boys' songs himself, and he joins forces and co-writes lots of the others. A favourite one is from the Crazy Horses Album, 'Utah'. That's one of Merrill's. He was thrilled to bits when he heard that the New Seekers were doing so well with it.

One of the things he most dislikes is listening to the group's old discs. When he's feeling down in the dumps he reads his fan mail to cheer him up.

"We owe such a lot to our fans," he says, "and they write such super, marvellous letters, that I really get a lift going through them all from time to time." Merrill says that his main ambition is to keep singing and playing with the group for the rest of his life, and to work together with Mary on their house so that it's just exactly as they want it to be. But as well as that, he says that he'd like to produce films or records on a part-time basis, too.

So Merrill, for one, is going to have a very busy future.

LET ME IN

Lovin' you could be so easy,
Loving you could make me warm.
Ever since the day I left you,
I try but I just can't get you
Out of my mind.

Thought that I could do without you,
Thought that I had to look around,
But now that I know I need you,
And promise that I'll never leave you
Won't you please,

Let me in,
Let me in your arms again,
Let me give my love to you once more,
Let me love you, let me love you.

Take me in,
Take me in your arms to stay,
And I'll never go away again,
'Cause I love you, 'cause I love you.

I'll never be the same without you,
If I have to say goodbye,
I have no right to ask you
But if you can, won't you try to
Love me,
(Won't you try to love me)
Help me
(I need you so badly)
And let me (and let me)

Let me in, let me in your arms again,
Let me give my love to you once more,
Oh, 'cause I love you, 'cause I love you.

Oh, take me in,
Take me in your arms to stay,
And I'll never go away again,
Oh, 'cause I love you, 'cause I love you.

Oh, let me in, let me in your arms again,
Let me give my love to you once more,
Oh, let me love you, let me love you,
Take me in,
Take me in your arms to stay,
And I'll never go away.

© Kolob Music, USA   M. Osmond

16

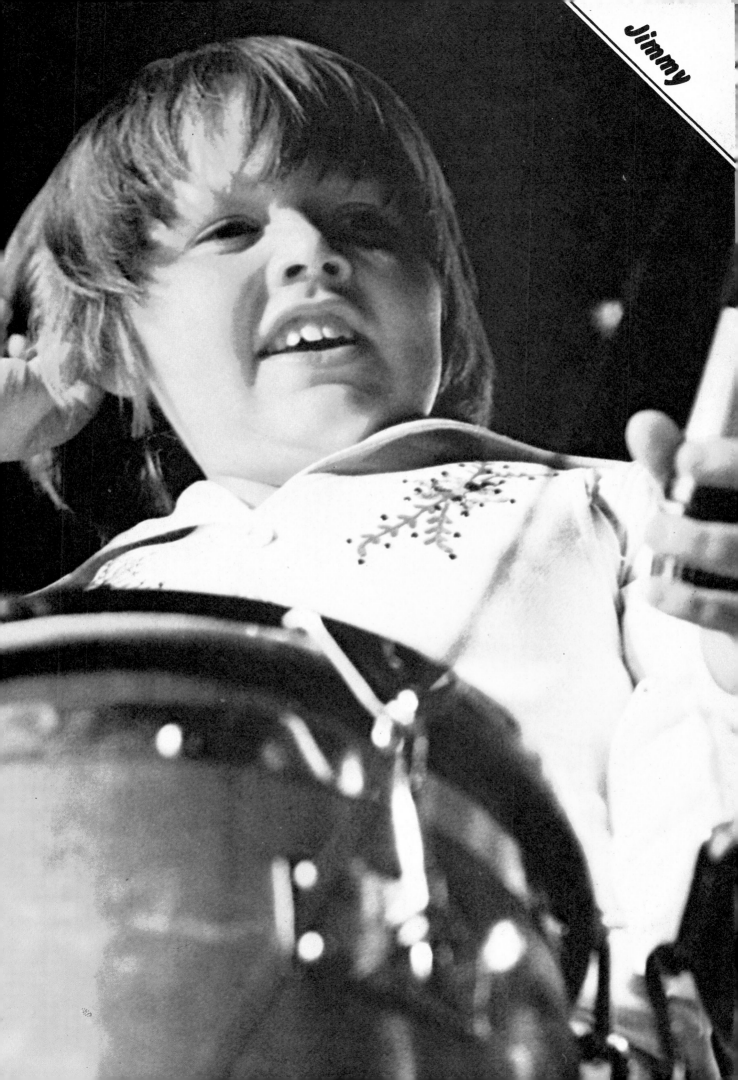

Alan

Marie & Jimmy

Donny

FAN CLUB

Hello there,

I don't suppose I need to introduce myself to many of you, but for those of you who don't know me from a bar of soap, let me give you the lowdown.

My name is Maureen, and I run the official fan club for the Osmonds in Great Britain and Europe. I formed an information service on the Osmonds just after Donny released his chartbuster, *Puppy Love*, over here, because the GPO and broadcasting services were all beseiged by sacks of mail for the boys, not to mention the boys' recording company, Polydor, and all the pop magazines.

The family then asked me to form an official fan club, which I did right away. My office was absolutely snowed under with mail and requests for membership right from the very beginning, and even though the boys and their parents take a very active part in the running of the club, you can just imagine the fantastic amount of time and energy we all need to keep you all happy.

My local post office is really super. Every day they come to deliver and collect mail. Nearly every room in my house has had to take some of the overflow to accommodate all the bits and pieces I need to run the fan club. We don't keep the car in the garage any more — I'm afraid that's where we have to store all the fan club stationery. We don't eat in the dining room any more, either, as that is now used for storage too. Actually, the fact that the dining room has been pinched doesn't matter, 'cos we're all so busy dealing with fan mail at the office that we hardly have time to eat at home any more.

At Christmas time, on birthdays and Valentine's Day, visitors have a problem even getting up the stairs to the office door, for the sacks and sacks of cards and letters for the boys reach right into the corridor. Believe me, they all get forwarded on to the States, where the boys really do read them.

As well as dealing with mail to, from, and about the boys, the fan club does other things, too.

We have a pen pal service for members who would like to hear from fans in this country and in Europe.

There are exciting things like T-shirts, scarves, bags and Donny caps available exclusively to fan club members, and many other surprises, too.

If any of you want to write to any of the boys personally, I shall be only too pleased to pass on your letters. Put your membership number on the top left-hand corner of the envelope, and I will forward on all mail every week. Mail to the States and back takes a bit of time, so don't lose heart if you have to wait a long time for a reply.

If you aren't already a member and feel that you'd like to be part of our big, big happy family, drop me a line at Osmonds Fan Club Europe, London, W1A 4YE. All I need is your full name, full postal address, and a self-addressed and stamped envelope. I don't want you to send me any money, please. As soon as you have been enrolled as one of our members you will receive a fan club biography book giving stacks of information about the boys, a full colour poster of the group, an autographed photo with a welcoming message, and your own membership card (the annual subscription is 75 pence). There is also an exclusive Osmonds' Secret Code card, a metal pin badge, a colour postcard of the group, a newsletter which you will receive quarterly, and three newsletter vouchers and envelopes to exchange regularly.

If you are not already one of us, I do hope you'll be getting in touch with me soon.

Bye for now,
Sincerely,

Maureen
Secretary.

Maureen

Donny

It all began with a spot at McCormicks when Donny was only four year old – his very first booking. In those days the boys didn't have any hit records of their own, and they used to perform other people's music at supper clubs and cabaret.

Then, in 1970, the brothers were signed up, plus Donny, by MGM, and things really began to swing. With the release of their first record, *One Bad Apple*, came over 5,000 fan letters a week – all for Donny, who read them all! Early in 1971, they made their first album, which included Donny's *Sweet and Innocent*, and Donny really had arrived on the pop scene with a bang.

There have always been lots of rumours circulating around Donny, especially every time he makes a solo disc. Will he be leaving the group and going out on his own? You bet your sweet life he won't. Although he loves singing solo, he says he is part of a big happy family, and it's staying that way.

He didn't really become famous in Britain until *Puppy Love* in 1972. Well, success hasn't gone to his head at all, as you might expect. The only thing that's changed about Donny over the years is his voice, which has become a few tones deeper, and more mature. Donny says: "Sure, I'm getting older, and so is everyone else, too. The nice thing about growing older together is that no one gets left behind. So even though there may be a change in my singing style over the years, I hope that this will be matched by a corresponding growing maturity of my fans, too. I like to think that my fans are growing with me."

Donny is very conscious of the feelings his fans have for him. On an early British tour, you may remember that all the boys one by one caught a nasty flu virus. Donny was so worried at the thought of his fans' disappointment that he managed to persuade his doctor to get him to the theatre by ambulance in time for the show.

Donny is one of those lucky people who feels happy whatever age he is. He says that whatever age he's been, he's never wished to be younger or older, or different – except when he gets a few pimples! He enjoys every minute. He does school work still, although with all the amount of moving around the family does he can't actually go to a proper school. This is where Mary comes in handy, with her training as a teacher. His favourite 'school' book is *Fundamentals of Electricity*, because he is very keen on electronics. His bedroom has to be seen to be believed, and I wouldn't be at all surprised if he ends up being technical adviser on a computerised James Bond-type movie one day! He says that his interest in electronics began when he was a baby. Crawling around the floor one day he got a bit too curious and poked his finger into a socket, which gave him a shock. Since then he's been hooked on electricity!

Donny likes to go to the cinema, and has seen a lot of films. Sometimes the family has film shows at home, and Donny loves to settle down in front of a good movie.

He tends to watch a lot of television, too, especially when the family is on tour or doing a cabaret, because there's a lot of time spent just waiting around backstage. In fact, anyone who goes backstage to meet the boys before a show will always find Donny glued to the box. The trouble is, that when you are all keyed up and waiting to go on, there's not much you can concentrate on. So television passes the time easily. Donny never goes to bed immediately after a show, either, because it takes him so long to wind down after a performance. Normally he likes to get an early night when he's not working on shows.

He spends a lot of time in his bedroom, even when he's not sleeping. Did you know that he has a bed that disappears into the ceiling? Most of the time he spends in his room is taken up with his inventions, but now and then he slopes off for a little session of song writing. He doesn't think his brothers would think much

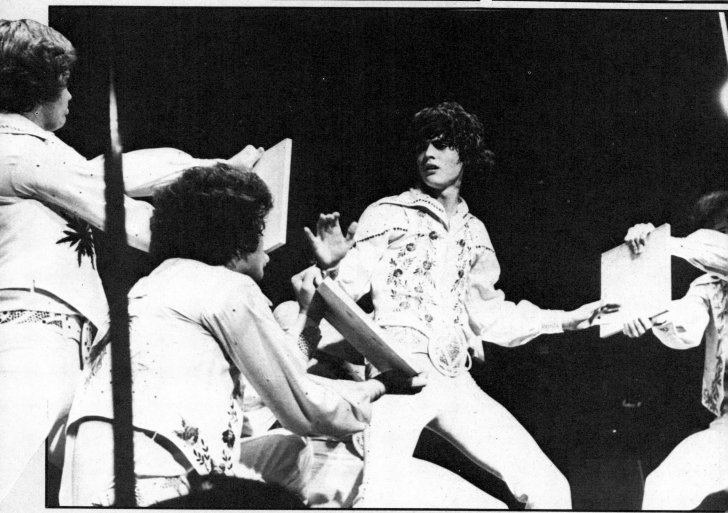

of his efforts, however, so he hasn't tried to plug any of his musical ideas.

Although he admits to being a bit of a daydreamer, he says he never daydreams when he's on stage. "I always think about the message of the songs we are singing, or concentrate on the routine," he says. And it's just as well, because sometimes it's a bit hard carrying on with the performance when there's a lot of reaction from the audience. There are good moments and bad. One of the worst ones was when they were doing a date in the south and it was very, very hot. There were thousands of fans pushing forward in the hope of touching Donny, and the safety barrier was only a small wooden fence! Phew!

Once, when they were touring Canada, a great wave of fans came rushing towards them as they got into their car. If they hadn't managed to get the car going quickly, Donny says he's sure the family would have ended up in hospital, very, very squashed. "I was frightened," he said, "but I think I actually enjoyed it, too."

He says that one of his great nightmares is that any of his fans may get hurt. He worries about that a lot, and hates to see it happen. In fact, he feels so strongly about it that he is on record as saying once, after an accident to a fan, that if there was a danger of more accidents he would rather cancel his tour! He likes to hear them shouting for him when the boys are on stage. It doesn't seem to put him off at all. He still manages, in spite of all his commitments, to read most of his fan mail, although a lot of it has to wait a long time. He travels so much that by the time he gets home and sits down to read his fan letters, much of the news is out of date. He gets quite a number of poems as well as letters. Donny says: "I love poems, especially if they're sent to me, but I have to confess that I never learn any off by heart, and I've never tried to write any myself."

He has a special spot for his English fans and England. They're great. He's very proud of the fact that he met the Queen, too. He says the English are nice, and one of the nicest things about them is that they invented the mini skirt, his favourite fashion. As you know, Donny's all in favour of inventions.

The Osmonds love to go home

Having a full and busy life, the Osmonds don't have as much time as you or me for relaxing at home. Mind you, the family are lucky, because they always work together, so they see each other all the time. When they're on tour, or filming, a lot of the time is spent dashing around in cars and planes, with nights spent in hotels.

Hotels are fun, because they're usually full of other people you can get to meet, and the service is always great, 'cos all you have to do is ring a bell and ask for anything you want! But it is even nicer to get home, back to your own house, your own room, to be with your own things.

When the Osmonds aren't working hard, they love to get out to their ranch in Utah. Being at home is a time for relaxation, and catching up on all the things that get missed, like seeing friends and relations, and having real family get-togethers. If you ask any member of the family where they most like to be, the answer is always the same – Utah. Even when they realised that they would be spending a lot of time in other places, Mother and Father Osmond were determined to keep up a home in Utah, so that the family would always have a permanent base to operate from.

The Osmonds do all the things that other people do at home. But one of the things which makes them extra glad to be home is Mother's cooking! Mother has taught Marie how to cook, so the lucky man who gets her will be well fed! Mother makes fantastic home-baked bread and stews, and concocts great salads and snacks, and the family really look forward at the end of every trip to getting back. The Osmond kitchen is a huge affair, and there is plenty of room to store and prepare the food the family loves so well.

All the boys love salads. Mind you, that's not just a bunch of lettuce and a few hard boiled eggs, either. Each has his own particular favourite. Virl, for instance, likes a sweet salad, of fresh fruit and gelatine. Merrill's favourite is a mixture of sea food, vegetables and pasta. Here's how to make Merrill's special salad. You need:

1 cup of uncooked macaroni
½ pint of shrimps or prawns, shelled
1 cup of crabmeat, or tuna, cooked
1 carrot
1 tablespoon of peas
1 tablespoon of chopped green beans
Mayonnaise or salad cream for dressing

First heat the macaroni, peas and green beans in boiling, salted water, until cooked but still firm. Drain and cool. Chop the carrot and leave raw. Now place all the ingredients in a large bowl, add the mayonnaise or salad cream, and mix thoroughly. The salad can be kept in the fridge until required.

Alan, now, prefers a crisp green salad. You can make a salad like this very quickly. All you need is:

1 lettuce, nice and crisp
1 green pepper
1 tablespoon of oil
½ lemon, squeezed
1 celery stalk
few sprigs of watercress

Shred the lettuce; de-seed the pepper and chop finely; chop the celery into small pieces; then put these ingredients into a bowl, adding squeezed lemon and the oil. Mix well. Garnish with sprigs of watercress.

All the boys are nibblers sometimes, and get peckish between meals. When they are on tour, they fill up with peanuts, crisps and sandwiches. However, for nibbling at home, Mother makes a fine pâte, which is served with small triangles of toasted bread. One particular favourite is fish pâte, made from pilchards, which is very nutritious. Here's how to make it. You need:

1 can of pilchards (small size)
1 lemon
1 egg
salt and pepper
fresh cream, or milk, as required

Firstly, drain the pilchards. Then mash them, adding salt and pepper. If you want a very fine pâte, rub the pilchards through a sieve, or use a blender instead of mashing. Add the juice of half the lemon, and the egg. If the pâte is too dry, add the optional cream or milk. Serve with small triangles of toasted bread, and cut the other half of the lemon for those who like their pâte sharp.

Wayne is a big health food fan. He's not a crank, or a vegetarian, but he pays great attention to food values. He also likes a good, substantial meal, with plenty of flavour. One of his favourites is ham platter, because it contains all the most valuable foods, and has a strong flavour, too. For a ham platter for two people, you need:

½ lb of chopped ham, cooked
1 onion, sliced in rings
1 green pepper, de-seeded and cut in rings
1 red pepper, as above
1 pear
1 apple
1 teaspoon of mixed herbs
1 bay leaf
1 clove of garlic (if you like it)
pepper
oil for frying

Heat the oil in a heavy pan; add the onion and cook till golden; remove. Heat the peppers in the pan for three minutes, then remove. Put the garlic, herbs and ham into the pan and fry till the meat begins to brown. Transfer all ingredients into an ovenproof serving dish, surrounded with creamed potatoes, and place in the oven for 20 minutes to brown the potatoes.

All the boys, and Mary and Marie, and of course Father, too, love Mother's home-baked bread; in fact, Donny and Jimmy can't be shifted from the kitchen when Mother is baking bread. Mother's bread is so popular that she always makes at least three loaves each time. And I bet they all disappear quickly, too! Here is her recipe for rich home-made bread, which the boys would love everyone to know, it's so great:

3 lb of wholemeal flour
1 oz of yeast
1½ pints of milk
1 oz of butter
1 good teaspoon of salt
½ lb of honey
4 fl oz of olive oil, or other oil

Mix the yeast with ¼ pint of warmed water in a bowl and add one teaspoon of the honey. Put it in a warm place for about 15 minutes, or until a froth forms on top. Add the butter and honey to the warm milk in a large pan. Put the flour and salt into a large mixing bowl and add the yeast mixture. Gradually add the milk mix until a dough is made. Then add the oil. Turn on to a floured board and knead it thoroughly for at least 10 minutes. Then put it in a warm place in a floured bowl to rise to double its original size – this will take about 45 minutes if the temperature is warm enough. Then knead again, and divide into three. Place each piece into a greased and floured 1 lb loaf tin. Leave for a while in the warm to rise again. Place in an oven at 475 degrees for 15 minutes, then reduce the heat to 375 degrees for about 20 minutes, or until the bread is crusty and browned.

Mmmmmmmm!!! Makes your mouth water just thinking about it, doesn't it? I can understand why the family loves it when Mother has a baking day!

FAMILY TREE OF MR. OSMOND

George Osmond
m
Nancy Canham

Frederick Jacobsen
m
Elizabeth Peterson

William Hoy
m
Agens Burrell

Isaac Hawk Vial
m
Terisha Ann Beelar

George Osmond m Amelia Jacobson

Thomas van Hoy m Martha Terisha Vial

Rulon Osmond m Agnes van Hoy

George Virl Osmond
m
Olive May Davis

Virl
m
Chris

Tommy
m
Lynn

Alan

Wayne

Merrill
m
Mary

Jay

Donny

Marie

Jimmy

FAMILY TREE OF MRS. OSMOND

Thomas J. Davis
m
Elizabeth Williams

John Martin
m
Ann Jenkins

William Nichols
m
Ellen White

John Booth
m
Ann Lythgoe

Samuel W. Davis m Mary Ann Martin

Benjamin T. Nichols m Olive Booth

Thomas Martin Davis m Vera Ann Nichols

Olive May Davis
m
George Virl Osmond

The Osmonds haven't always been American. Did you know that some of them came originally from London, some from Denmark, some from Scotland, South Wales, Middlesex, Durham, and Lancashire? On Mr Osmond's side of the family, George Osmond, who is the first person to appear on the family tree, came from somewhere in London, and was born some time around 1800. He married a Londoner, too. Their son married a Danish girl, Amelia Jacobsen, although by this time they were in America. Mr Osmond's great-grandfather on his father's side was a Scot, from Greenock, Scotland, who married in America.

On Mrs Osmond's side of the family, there are more foreigners, too, because all of her great-grandparents were from Britain.

Why don't you try to trace your great-great-grandparents? You may find that you have all sorts of foreign connections, too.

DISCOGRAPHY

Singles

1971 One bad apple/He ain't heavy, he's my brother
Double lovin'/Chilly winds
Yo yo/Keep on my side

1972 Down by the lazy river/He's the light of the
world
Hold her tight/Love is
Crazy horses/Are you up there?

1973 Let me in/One way ticket to anywhere

1974

DONNY

1971 Sweet and innocent/Flirtin'
Go away little girl/Time to ride
Hey girl/I knew you when

1972 Puppy love/Let my people go
Too young/Love me
Why?/Lonely boy

1973 Twelfth of never
Young Love/A million to one
When I fall in love/Are you lonesome tonight?

1974

MARIE

1973 Paper roses/

1974

JIMMY

1971 If Santa were my daddy/Silent night

1972 Mother of mine/Long haired lover from
Liverpool
Tweedle dee/Mama'd know what to do

Albums

1971 Osmonds (not released here)
Home made (not released here)
Phase III
The Donny Osmond album (Donny)
To you with love (Donny)

1972 The Osmonds live
Crazy horses
Portrait of Donny (Donny)
Too young (Donny)
My best to you (Donny) (not available here)
Mother of mine (Jimmy)
Little Jimmy Osmond – Killer Joe (Jimmy)

1973 The Plan
Alone together (Donny)
A time for us (Donny)
Paper roses (Marie)

OSMOND FOUNDATION

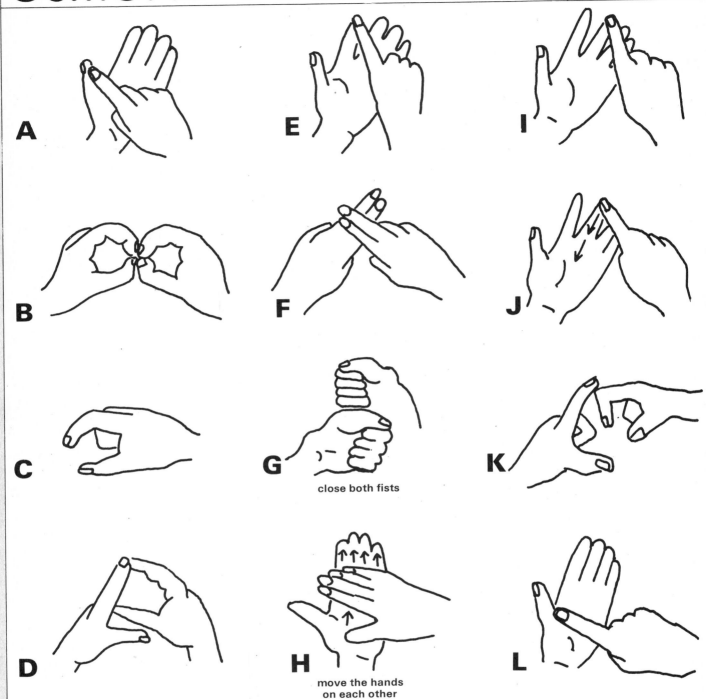

A

E

I

B

F

J

C

G
close both fists

K

D

H
**move the hands
on each other**

L

Eldest Osmond brothers Virl and Tommy were born with severe hearing disorders, and Mrs Osmond had a problem on her hands. She was told by specialists not to waste money on hearing aids, but she went ahead, and purchased glasses with hearing aids.

Well-meaning friends told her that sign language was a waste of time. However, she taught Tommy and Virl sign language. She used a record machine, and even a vacuum cleaner, to develop for the boys a relationship between movement of lips and the vibration of sound. She was sure, she says, that anyone can improve knowledge in the right way, and in 1966 the boys were called to go to their mission, which was the best possible way of proving her point!

Virl and Tommy together were responsible for organising and instructing classes in the teaching of sign language to over two hundred people that year. They succeeded, as their mother had, years earlier, by ignoring proven methods for working with deaf children by bringing a combination of common sense, love, instinct and imagination into the process of education.

In 1972 the Osmond Foundation was formed to help blind and deaf children.

Nowadays, Tommy teaches deaf children in a school in Salt Lake City, as well as helping to organise and supervise the international fan club.

Virl attends Brigham Young University in Utah, and at the same time spends considerable time

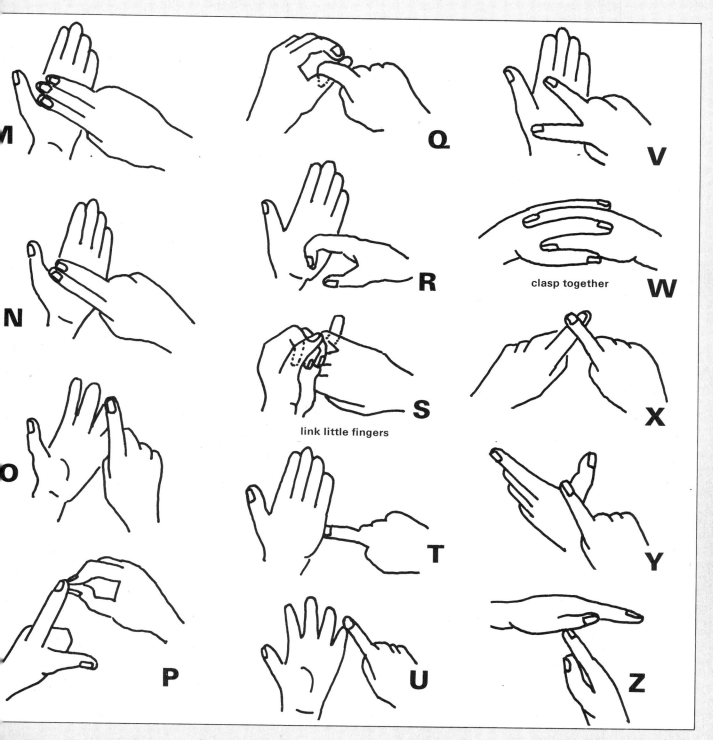

M

N

O

P

Q

R
link little fingers
S

T

U

V

clasp together
W

X

Y

Z

working for the Osmond Foundation.

The object of the Osmond Foundation is to provide encouragement, equipment, and the means necessary for the education of deaf and blind children. Mrs Osmond is the President of the Foundation.

All the other members of the family are very deeply involved in it.

Because the two oldest boys were born deaf, the rest of the family have all learned to communicate through using sign language. And very expert at it they are, too.

How about learning some sign language yourself?

Perhaps you know someone who is deaf and dumb that you could communicate with in this way. You never know, it might come in handy if you lose your voice.

If you meet any of the Osmonds you can always try talking to them in sign language.

There are two ways of using sign language; one is to use signals which can mean a whole word or phrase. The other way is to use the manual alphabet, which means that you have to spell out the words. As a matter of fact, the English two-handed system of sign language is not used in the States. So if you want to talk to the boys in deaf and dumb language you may as well stick to the manual alphabet system, which is universal, and spell the words out. You don't have to have a teacher, you can learn the alphabet from the drawings here.

MARIE THE OTHER OSMOND

When Jimmy told reporters that his sister was about to have her first single released, their recording company was beseiged by callers and letters wanting details. That was before anyone had even heard it.

Marie had been experimenting in the studios, but no one had actually thought of putting any of her tapes out, at that stage. But it wasn't long before her first single, *Paper Roses*, was released over here, followed by her 'Paper Roses' album.

Marie had felt envious of her brothers for some time. There she was, travelling with them on their tours, and always wishing that it was her the fans were waiting for when the boys went on stage. She spends a lot of time with her brothers, and has picked up a lot of the experience of an artiste on tour, so facing her first audience wasn't such a difficult thing when she finally got around to it. Waiting in the wings was agony for her, as the excitement built up before each show.

Jimmy, years younger, already had a solo spot in the act, and Marie was very pleased when at last she was able to join her brothers.

Why did she stay in the wings for so long? Well, Mother and Father figured that a girl should be a bit older before she starts work. Also, they had to be sure that she had talent before they put her out there. They didn't want her to be a star just because she was the Osmonds' sister, but because she was good enough herself.

"That's all I ever wanted to do," said Marie. "I had studied shorthand and typing, and I still keep it up, of course, because it is always useful to have a second string to your bow, so to speak."

Marie has terrific respect for her brothers' energy, and doesn't see herself jumping around on stage the way they do. Her favourites are ballads and romantic songs, with an orchestral backing.

Nearest in age to Donny, she spends a lot of her time with him, and they confide their problems and worries to each other.

Fame doesn't worry her. She says her brothers are a wonderful example of how normal you can remain even though you are a superstar. She says: "It's a great help being part of a big, happy family. If any one of us gets a bit big headed, the others soon bring him (or her!) down to size."

Even before she cut her first disc she was a bit of a celebrity. She has her own magazine columns, and her own brand of natural, organic make-up. In fact, one of her main interests apart from the show business part of their lives, is make-up.

She takes a lot of trouble with her make-up, although she doesn't pretend to be a great expert. She told me, "One day, when I went out for a dinner with my family, I decided I'd go mad and pop on a pair of false eyelashes. You see, I'd never tried them before, it was a bit of an experiment. The boys were all getting impatient and ready to go, so I hurried my make-up, and didn't really follow the instructions properly. Well, there we all were, eating our first course, when Jimmy yelled 'Look Mother there's a spider in my soup.' My grown-up poise was completely shattered when the waiter fished my eyelashes out of Jimmy's soup. You see, the glue hadn't had time to dry properly, so, flip, flop, off they came! It certainly taught me a lesson, I can tell you."

quiz !

Just imagine that you had all the Osmonds to choose from for a boy-friend. Which one would you choose? Of course, they're all great guys, and you probably have your favourite. But to have a successful relationship with someone doesn't just depend on how much you like them. It always helps to have something in common with your boyfriend. After all, you don't want to be carted off to everlasting football matches by him if you are really a bookish, stay-at-home girl. And you are not going to like watching old films on the television night after night if you are a get-up-and-go girl!

Here is a very lighthearted quiz to see which of the boys would be best for you, though don't take it too seriously.

But don't get too upset if you don't get the one you like best of all. Opposites have been known to attract!

1. WHAT SORT OF FOOD DO YOU ENJOY EATING MOST?

a. Casual snacks, no fuss or bother.
b. Hefty meals of ham and eggs.
c. Home cooking, and lots of it.
d. Exciting new dishes.
e. Sweet foods, especially cereals and puddings.
f. Fruit and nuts, and real orange juice.

2. WHAT KIND OF CLOTHES DO YOU FEEL HAPPIEST IN?

a. Pretty and feminine outfits.
b. Casual and practical clothes.
c. Glamorous creations.
d. Trendy up-to-the-minute styles.
e. Any thing as long as it fits.
f. Something different, just for a laugh.

3. WHICH BIRTHDAY PRESENT WOULD PLEASE YOU MOST?

a. Ticket for the World Cup Final.
b. A camera.
c. A cow for a pet.
d. Life membership to a film club.
e. Giant scrap book.
f. A practical joke kit.

4. YOU GET A CASH WINDFALL. WHAT WOULD YOU BUY?

a. Records.
b. Deep freeze.
c. A bakery.
d. Clothes.
e. An aeroplane.
f. A circus.

5. WHAT IS YOUR FAVOURITE COLOUR, OR COLOUR COMBINATION?

a. Lavender.
b. Yellow.
c. Green.
d. Black and red together.
e. Red and white.
f. Purple.

6. YOUR DATE ASKS YOU WHAT YOU'D LIKE TO DO. YOU SAY . . .

a. How about a walk, it's stopped raining now?
b. I know a nice quiet place where we can talk.
c. How about going down to the gym?
d. You decide . . . I like surprises.
e. Lets go to the youth club, there are lots of people there.
f. Why don't we stay in, there's an old film on the box tonight.

7. WHAT IS YOUR PET HATE?

a. Homework.
b. Being young, or small.
c. Planning ahead.
d. Being asked not to fidget.
e. Late nights.
f. Old, scratchy records.

8. WHICH SPORT, IF ANY, DO YOU LIKE MOST?

a. Swimming.
b. Football.
c. Walking.
d. Chess.
e. Gymnastics.
f. None. You'd rather help with the decorating.

9. WHAT DO YOU MOST ENJOY READING?

a. Letters.
b. Poetry.
c. Newspapers.
d. Romantic novels.
e. Thrillers.
f. Travel books.

10. WHAT SORT OF PERSON ARE YOU?

a. Gregarious.
b. Responsible and serious.
c. Fidgety.
d. Humorous.
e. Lively.
f. Domesticated.

HERE'S HOW YOU SCORE

Q.	a	b	c	d	e	f
1.	5	2	6	4	3	1
2.	5	2	1	3	6	4
3.	6	1	2	5	3	4
4.	1	5	6	3	2	4
5.	3	1	2	4	6	5
6.	2	1	6	4	3	5
7.	5	6	4	2	1	3
8.	6	4	2	1	5	3
9.	3	4	1	6	2	5
10.	3	1	2	4	6	5

How did you do?

Score 15 points or below: You and Alan will have a lot in common. If you ever do get to meet him you will probably find there'll be lots to talk about. If you scored exactly 10, then you really are Alan's soul-mate. He hates staying up late, so don't get too keen on the late night horror film on telly – you'll be up by yourself, with no one to cling to in the creepy scenes. His favourite drink is freshly squeezed oranges, and lots of them. So I'd go out and swop mum's old coffee percolator for an electric juicer if I were you. Still, if you lived in California you'd find it easier on the housekeeping, 'cos that's where the oranges grow! Hope you're not too much of a chatterbox. Because if you are, Alan might give you the old beady eye if you keep on going when he's in the throes of writing one of his songs. If you and Alan hit it off you're going to need lots of shelf space for storing all your picture albums – he's a very keen photographer. If you're the sort of girl who likes a man to be the boss, Alan's the one for you, as he likes to keep an eye on things and make all the decisions.

Score 16–25: Let's hope you're the adventurous type, for Wayne is sure to want to take you up in his plane. No room for nerves or vertigo. When he's not working he's usually fixing his plane. You should invest in a good strong washing machine to cope with all those greasy overalls he'll be bringing home. Wherever you went with Wayne you would never feel too homesick or out of touch, because he likes a good English breakfast of bacon and eggs to start the day right. You might introduce him to bubble and squeak and black pudding. He'd like that. I hope you're a dab hand at letter writing – Wayne hates it, and he'll get you to do it for him if he can. When you're apart you needn't expect too much in the way of mail from him, either. Best thing would be to get yourself a tape recorder so that you can send tapes to each other instead of letters.

Score 26–35: You're sure to get along with Merrill, 'cos he's a very friendly and sincere person, like you. He loves meeting new people, and he's easy to get to know well. Don't for heavens sake invite him home to see or hear your treasured collection of the boys' old discs. If there's one thing bound to send him off in the other direction, but quickly, it's their old records. He likes his drinks with lots of ice, so remember to get the fish fingers out of the fridge and put in lots of ice trays instead!

Score 36–45: If your answers added up to Jay's score, you're in for a rave up. He may drive you mad sometimes, for a few of his jokes are so old and hairy that you probably heard them while you were still in your playpen! You'll never be bored, for he's always got something up his sleeve. If you can cope with endless jokes and puns, apple-pie beds, bags of flour over the door, joke cushions, itching powder and plastic spiders, then you've come to the right place. Jay loves giving surprises and being surprised, but you'll need to be bright to keep one step ahead of him. Going out with Jay can be noisy and sometimes crowded, since he hates fan dodging, and will always stop – given a chance – for his fans to talk to him. If he comes home to meet Mum and Dad, warn them to put the best family heirlooms out of sight, including their good furniture – Jay's liable to beat out rhythms on anything. Beware, he might knock pounds off the artistic value of your Mum's best Formica kitchen table!

Score 46–55: Boy, oh boy. So your score gets into dreamboat Donny's range. Anyone who gets Donny is going to be the envy of all his fans. But don't get carried away. He expects his dream girl to be able to cook as well as Mother, look as good as sister Marie, and be as interesting and nice as his brothers. What a lot to live up to! Still, you won't have to pay any bills for servicing or repair of electrical gadgets, 'cos Donny's an electrical genius. He'll have your broken record player going again before you can say 'disc'. And you never know, he might even invent a robot to do all the housework for you, so that you have lots of time left to prepare his favourite snack – doorstep 'ploughman's lunch', great big cheese sandwiches. And you'll be able to catch up on all those old silent movies which were made before your time – Donny thinks they're great.

Score 56–60: Well, Jimmy's not actually old enough to have dates yet, but he's well worth waiting for. And while you're waiting for him to grow up, get your hand in learning the fine art of home baking. He just love's fresh, straight-from-the-oven home-made bread. And when you finally do get him, try and get him to steer clear of Japan. For there he is a superstar in his own right, and has many, many eager fans, all waiting to grab him for themselves! Failing that, go with him. The change'll do you good, and you can keep all those eager Japanese girls away from him, too!

Score 65 or more: Well, I don't know how you did it, but you must have been cheating – admit it! Which shows you've got initiative, and nerve. And you'll probably have no trouble getting to meet them all, soon.

Marie

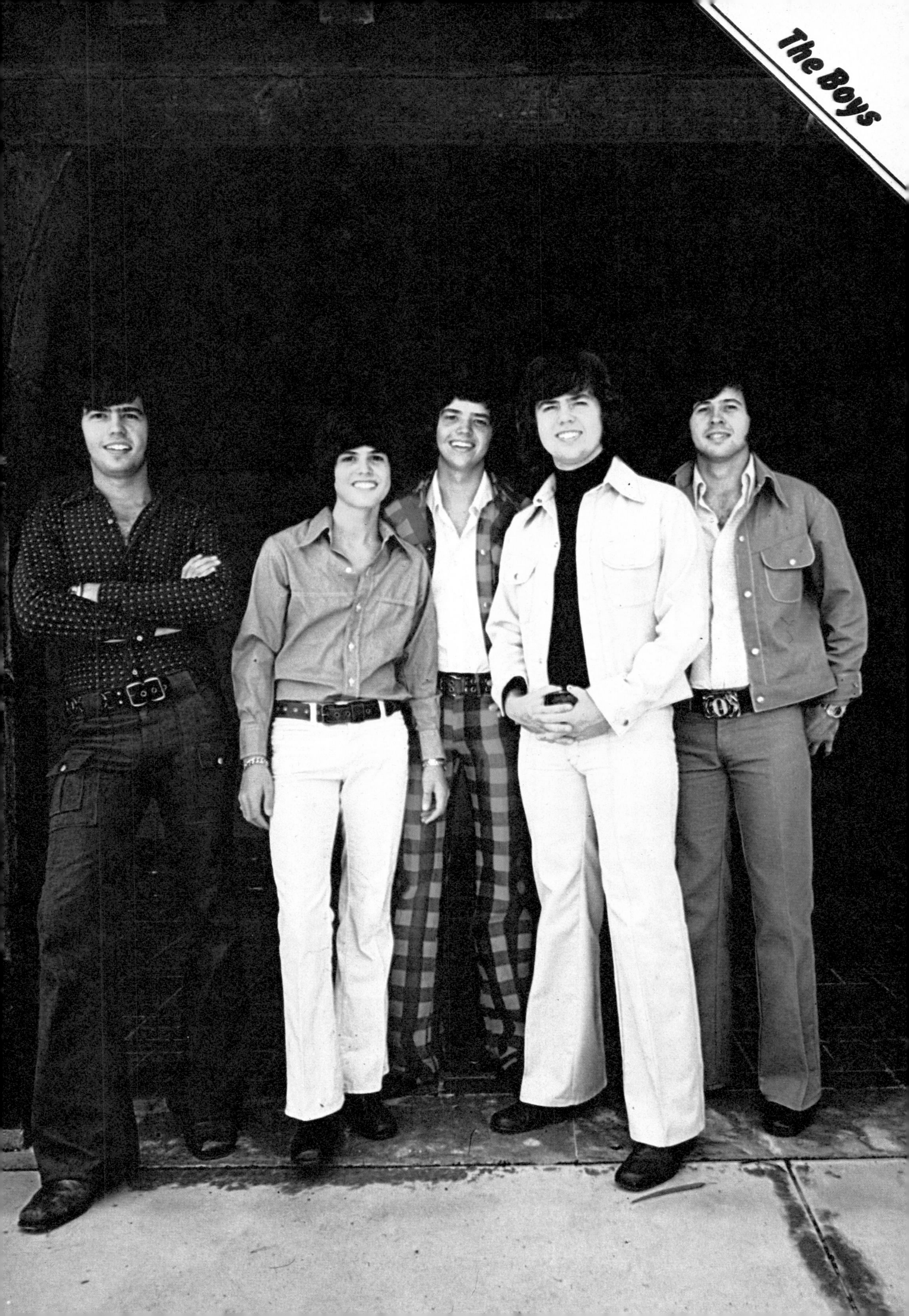

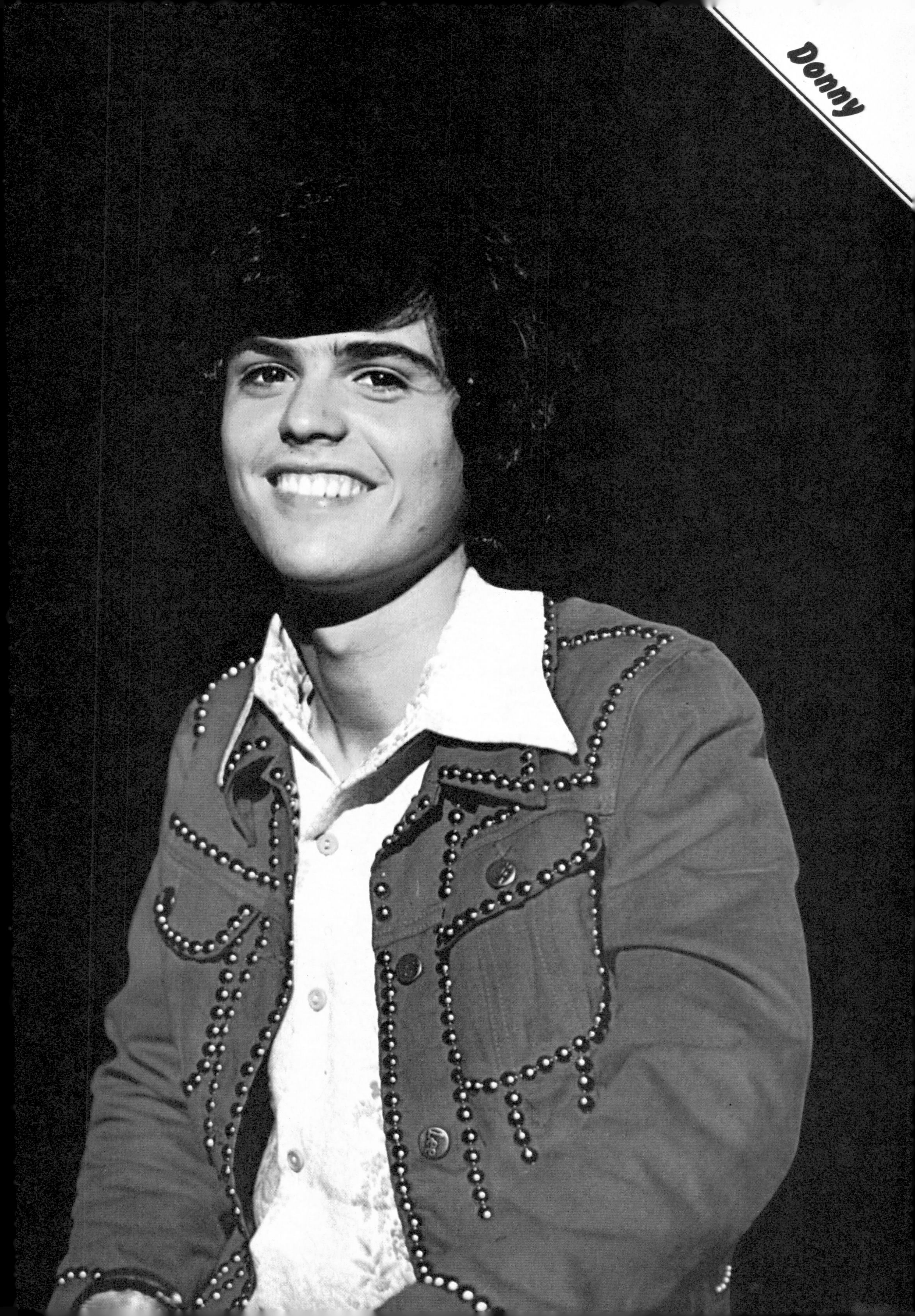

Donny

Jimmy

JAY, the joker of the pack

Jay's a card! He's always telling jokes. You should hear some of them, too. The family often tell him that most of his jokes should be drawing a pension, they're so old.

The greatest love in Jay's life has always been his drums; he first began showing an interest in percussion when he was only five years old, and was like a cat with two tails when he was given his first real drum kit.

Like his brothers, Jay has never had proper lessons in music, which means he has picked it up along the way. He seems to have a natural talent for rhythm, and so perhaps formal instruction would have been redundant in his case. Other pop musicians like to have Jay along as a 'session' drummer, and he is well known and respected in his own right as a drummer throughout the profession.

Jay has three drum kits, although one of them always stays at home. The drums he uses in his act have been wired so that they actually light up on stage. I wonder which electronics expert thought that one up?

Have you ever noticed the way Jay holds his drum sticks while he's playing? Watch closely next time you see him perform, and see if you can spot it!

Wouldn't it be great if Jay could make a solo release? Just drums. Well, it has been known; others have done it in the past, so there's no reason to think that it's impossible.

Jay made his first appearance with the singing Osmonds at the age of seven years. Fantastic, isn't it, to think that at seven he was going to the television studios after he'd finished school work. What were you doing at that age? I bet you can't even remember.

As well as playing the drums and singing with the group, Jay also plays the banjo and the saxophone. One of his favourite pastimes is training the Osmonds' dog, a Japanese Akita, called Fuji, who was given to the family when they toured Japan. Unfortunately, the family spends so much time away from home off on tours that Fuji has had to be fostered out to friends on a full-time basis, but Jay still goes over to their house and keeps up his relationship with Fuji.

As you will have heard, another of his favourite hobbies is collecting jokes. The less said about them, the better, some might say!

His favourite sports are football – the family has its own team, too; baseball, and watersports like surfing, skiing, swimming and sailing. Not that he gets much time for them.

He loves eating hamburgers and chocolate malts, and drinks gallons of orange juice.

A little bit on the shy side himself, Jay likes to meet people who are a bit shy, too, because he knows how they feel. However, he says, his ideal girl is not too shy, not too extrovert, with a great sense of humour to appreciate his jokes however feeble they are, and who enjoys the simple things in life such as a comfortable home, home cooking and long walks in the country.

Did you know that they've just invented rubber yarn for knitting so that dropped stitches will bounce back.

Some TV shows are very moving, aren't they?
Yes. They make me want to move away.

How should a successful garage advertise for customers? May we have the next dents?

We found a popular picnic spot which must be fabulous. After all, a million ants can't all be wrong!

Woman in shop: Is this fur okay in the rain?
Assistant: Madam, have you ever seen a rabbit carrying an umbrella?

Some people's idea of keeping a secret is to refuse to say who told it to them.

When your hotel advertises running water in all rooms, make sure it's not running through a leaking roof.

Whatever happened to the piglet who wanted to play Shakespeare?
He ended up as a hamlet.

Air companies are now allowing easy payment plans on fares so that all their passengers may be debt-propelled.

1st man: I have to earn my living by my wits.
2nd man: Well, half a living is better than none.

Teacher: Can you stand on your head?
Johnny: No, it's too high.

What is your psychiatrist doing these days? Mine's currently raisin' nuts.

Mother badger to mischievous baby badger: Stop badgering me!

Why do dogs wear more clothes in summer than in winter?
In winter they wear coats. And in summer they wear coats and pants.

What do you do with a hurt lemon?
Give it lemonade of course.

Why do some cows wear bells?
'Cos their horns aren't working.

What can you make out of banana skins?
Slippers.

What is the quickest way to double your money?
Fold it.

There's only one sort of jam I can't eat, and that's a traffic jam.

Did you know about the musician who spent all his time in bed?
Yeah. He wrote sheet music.

What do you know?

How much do you think you know about the Osmonds? Don't look now, but the answers are on page 77.

1. What was the title of Jimmy's first single?
2. Where were Merrill and Mary married?
3. Where is Donny's favourite 'think' place?
4. Do the boys ever answer fan mail personally?
5. How many of the Osmonds are left-handed?
6. Which ones?
7. Who, or what, is Fuji?
8. What are the names of the three Osmond wives?
9. What position does Merrill hold in the Mormon faith?
10. When is Mrs Osmond's birthday?
11. What is Tom and Virl's second language?
12. When are their birthdays?
13. Who makes the Osmonds' stage costumes?
14. Who sings the lyrics in *Proud Mary*?
15. All the boys have special belts – what for?
16. What was Marie's first release?
17. How many spaces for baby's initials did Mrs Osmond make on the family christening robe?
18. For how long did the boys receive professional music training?
19. The boys drink root beer, but they don't drink beer. Explain.
20. When and where was Donny's first professional engagement?

I sat in the train, watching the countryside slip by, mile by mile; it was cold outside, colder than I'd ever remembered before. The snow lay thick on the surrounding downs, giving the scenery a sort of sugar frosting. Luckily the warm compartment was empty, so I was able to spread myself out and read my book in comfort. I reminded myself that before long I'd have to think about moving a bit nearer the television studios where I worked as a secretary. The journey wasn't unpleasant, but it was very tiring travelling to and fro each day – especially in winter. I remembered that my boss had asked me to get in a bit earlier than usual this morning because we had some important scripts coming in which would have to be checked and typed urgently. I hoped that I was going to be able to make it – the weather wasn't improving.

It was all hustle and bustle at the studio when I finally arrived. Alan, the floor manager, was buzzing around waving his hands about temperamentally.

"Oh, thank heavens, Julie," he gasped, grabbing me by the elbow. "At last someone from production has arrived. Half the people who are meant to be here have got stuck out in the wilds of nowhere, waiting for the trains to get back to normal. We've got a whole crowd of people here for the gala show, and not enough hands to look after them. Be a love, and pop across to the dressing rooms. See what you can do, eh?"

My heart sank. I had hoped to slip into my office and get all that typing up-to-date before my boss got in. Those scripts were due to be typed, and the show went into rehearsals tomorrow, too. However, I went on down to the dressing rooms.

The chaos was unimaginable. Artistes and make-up girls were dashing around all over the place. I checked a few of the names on the doors. There were singers and musicians, dancers and comedians. The end section was just labelled 'Osmonds'. What a well kept secret! There I was, working right in the production office, and even I hadn't heard that the Osmonds were among the star-studded cast for our pop spectacular.

I was standing there just wondering which direction to offer help first, when one of the doors opened, and a cheeky looking boy poked his head out of the dressing room.

"Hi!," he said, "I'm stuck here half dressed and there's a button off my jacket. Could you ask my mother if she can come and help, please? Oh, by the way – I'm Jimmy Osmond."

"Hello, I'm Julie," I smiled. "Sure, hang on a moment and I'll go and look".

Off I went in search of Mrs Osmond. I found her eventually with the director, discussing the boys' act for the show. They looked very involved, and I didn't think I should interrupt just then. So I went along to the wardrobe mistress and borrowed a sewing kit.

Jimmy was delighted when I offered to do his jacket for him. Just as I was finished, there was a knock on the dressing room door and in walked Donny. It took all my self control to stand there and not look too silly. My heart was pounding madly. I felt sure that everyone could hear it, even above the chaotic jamboree outside. But Donny didn't seem to have noticed anything strange, and he smiled right at me in a frank and friendly manner as we managed introductions. He soon put me at ease. He told me that he'd been feeling a bit nervous about the programme, which was going out live. So he came along to see how Jimmy was feeling, too. We all sat down and were soon chatting away nineteen to the dozen, as they say.

I found myself telling them all about my family of four brothers who are all mad about football; my father and mother, who are super; our two huge sheepdogs, who are soppy; three cats, two goldfish, and one solitary rabbit. Donny said that he felt a bit sorry for the rabbit, 'cos it was all on its own, and the others all had someone else to keep them company. I was very happy to see that they thought it was all great, because I thought that maybe my

Date with a

life might be a bit boring for such sophisticated people like pop stars to listen to. Donny and Jimmy told me all about their ranch in America, where they kept beef cattle, and lots of horses, and about their two dogs who have to be fostered by neighbours because they are away on tour so often.

Suddenly the door burst open, and we were surrounded by the rest of his family. We had been sitting around chatting for over an hour, and it was time to get along to the set for a camera rehearsal. There wasn't much time for anything more than very brief greetings and introductions before they all dashed off down the corridor on to the set.

Mrs Osmond turned, saying, "It was very kind of you to fix Jimmy's suit like that, Julie. Thank you very much. Come on, let's see how they get on." And tucking her arm in mine, we went together to the set.

Well, needless to say, the show went off very well, but I didn't see much of them after it, because there were photo sessions and press interviews, and I went home thinking how lovely it had been meeting them.

The next day there was a huge bunch of flowers on my desk at the studio, with a short message which read "How about dinner? D." At first I thought that it must be a joke, until the phone rang, and it was Donny asking me to dinner that evening with the family.

Well, I'm sure it won't surprise any of you to learn that I don't remember a single thing about that evening! I was so excited that I floated on a cloud for days afterwards.

Then their English tour was over, and they had to go back to the States. But every day, Donny rang me and told me what the boys were doing,

what they'd been recording, and how they all were – including the cattle, horses and the two dogs! Those phone calls must have cost him a fortune.

One day, after Donny had finished speaking, Mrs Osmond came on the line and asked to speak to my mother. I couldn't hear what they said, but my mother came back into the sitting room later and said that Mr and Mrs Osmond would be happy if I could spend a short holiday with them on their ranch in Utah. I was thrilled. The next four weeks were spent making arrangements to go, and finally I set off.

The flight was fantastic – Heathrow, London to Los Angeles by jumbo jet – and it was a marvellous experience. We had arranged that Wayne would pick me up at the airport and fly me in his small plane on to the family home in Utah. The seats in the jumbo jet were big and comfortable, and after a few hours I dozed off, lulled to sleep by the good food and romantic music in the cabin.

I was woken up later by a change of engine noise which meant we were soon coming in to land. Trembling with excitement I reached across to fix my safety strap, as instructed. Oh! No! With a thud my heart dropped into my boots. We had slowed down, and the first thing I saw out of the window was a large sign which read 'WATERLOO'.

With a great sense of disappointment I realised that I'd fallen asleep on the train, and it had all been a dream. My eyes filled with unshed tears, and I blindly made my way to the television studio to begin yet another routine day as a production office secretary.

It was all hustle and bustle at the studio when I finally arrived. Alan, the floor manager, was buzzing around waving his hands about temperamentally.

"Oh, thank heavens, Julie," he gasped, grabbing me by the elbow. "At last someone from production has arrived. Half the people who are meant to be here have got stuck out in the wilds of nowhere, waiting for the trains to get back to normal. We've got a whole crowd of people here for the gala show, and not enough hands to look after them. Be a love, and pop across to the dressing rooms. See what you can do, eh?"

My heart singing, I almost flew down to the dressing rooms. You never know who you might meet in a television studio these days. . . .

dreamboat

The women in the Osmond family are all pretty and poised, so the boys all have a very high standard to judge the girls they meet, as you can imagine. But even if you're not lucky enough to actually meet any of the boys yet, what about the boys that you do meet? A lot of men model their dream girls on standards set by their mothers or their sisters. How well would you rate on a date with a fab chap?

First impressions are very important. It doesn't do to be too keen or you'll frighten the poor boy away. On the other hand, don't try to play hard to get — after a hard day's work no boy wants to do much chasing around after a cool cat!

If it's your first date with him, neither of you probably knows much about the other. Of course, you want him to like you, but don't tell him your life story at length. Give him a chance to tell you what he's like. Listen.

Most boys are just as unsure of themselves as you, so you must keep the odd nervous giggle to yourself — otherwise he'll think you're laughing at him. Mind you, there's no harm having a good laugh if he says something funny, but don't fall over backwards.

So he's finally asked you to go out with him, but (and typically male) hasn't given you a clue

How not to drop

about what sort of place you're going to. Most men like their women pretty and feminine, but not too flash. It's always safer to underdo the dressing up bit, rather than to overdress. Donny, for instance, says he likes to see girls looking neat in skirts and sweaters. I'm sure that goes for a lot of boys, too. Take a look at your nails before you go, for no boy likes holding hands with a bunch of chewed-up stumps. And even if you hope that he's going to spend a lot of time looking deep into your eyes, check the state of your tights to make sure they're not full of snags and ladders.

A boy likes a girl to be well mannered, remembering to say please and thank you at the right moments.

If he's taking you to a restaurant where you don't understand the food, let him do the ordering — or ask his advice, at least. Don't worry about the knife and fork bit too much — just watch what he's doing with his! And when it comes to time to settle the bill, keep your purse firmly shut. He wouldn't have asked you out if he couldn't afford it. If you really feel that your evening out has left him flat broke, he won't be offended if you — later — manage to get tickets for a show he'd like. Even if he obviously can afford it, he'll be flattered. Anyway, it's an excuse to see him again!

clanger on a date

Right colour, right shape, you can look GREAT!

All the boys are proud to have a girl like Marie for a sister. Marie herself says that she likes to look nice, especially for her brothers. But, she says, she had a lot of help from Mother, who always looks good. Mother has a 'good eye' for picking out the right colour, or the right shape. Mother helps all the family when they go buying new clothes, and they always are glad to take her advice.

Marie is lucky, because she has a good figure which comes from eating all the right things. And if you've got a good shape you're likely to be able to wear more of the sort of clothes you like than if your figure is bad. If you've got a fantastic figure you won't need much help to find the right sort of clothes to suit you. But what about some help for those of you with a bit of a problem? Mother has a few tips for looking good which might be of help to make you into the sort of girls the boys are bound to like!

If you are a bit overweight, don't pick anything a bit on the tight side. Stay away from drab, pale colours, too, because they're fattening.

Go gay on accessories, especially on simple styles. Bracelets, bright hats and scarves, will dress any outfit up if the accessories are carefully chosen.

Avoid very small, or very large floral prints if your figure is less than perfect. And steer clear of trendy out-of-the-way fashions in what looks like upholstery material. You don't want to look like a three-seater sofa.

Short girls shouldn't wear belts, unless they are very slim, because they cut you in half.

Choose dresses in a good fabric that hangs well, and try to get all your clothes lined so that they fall better, and last longer. You may notice that the Osmonds always tend to go for soft, well-wearing materials, rather than stiff, formal and starchy fabrics. They all do a lot of travelling, and inter-

you can look GREAT !

views, in their ordinary day to day clothes, so their clothes above all must be good looking and comfortable. That's a good yardstick to bear in mind when buying clothes. Does it suit me? Is it comfortable? Is it suitable to meet people in? If the answer to any of these is no, then forget it, and try another shop!

All the boys like separates, and you will notice that Mary and Marie wear a lot of skirts matched up to tops, either blouses or sweaters.

The boys like suede and leather coats, and you may have noticed that they have leather and skin jackets themselves. They need a lot of looking after though, and they say that if you're not prepared to keep them in good condition you'll end up looking like a rocker rather than a fashion plate!

Simple, young clothes are favourites with the boys. As Donny says, leave the vamp styles to the vamps! Although the boys favourite styles are feminine looking, that doesn't mean you have to get rid of your slacks or jeans. On the contrary, the girls all wear slacks when they're on the ranch. After all, you can't fork hay or round up cattle in a frilly skirt — or can you!

What to do when the Osmonds drop in...

Imagine that you've just heard from the Osmonds Fan Club secretary that one of your letters to them was so nice that they'd like to pop round to your home for a visit, just to say a personal thank you. My! What a thought. Do you tell your mother and ask her to lay on a splendid spread? Or do you dash up to your room and do a bit of research for the occasion? Obviously, the boys would like it better if you managed everything without too much fuss and bother, I'm sure. But where do you start? Well, let's start at the top and work on down.

First of all – Alan. Like all the older ones, Alan is tall and well built. So remember to have enough strong, comfortable furniture around. If your chairs are spindly antique things, get them out of the way, or the boys won't feel comfortable. If you haven't got enough seats, try moving in one of the divan beds from the spare room – it'll make a very good sofa, if you add a few cushions and put it against the wall.

All the boys love home-made food, so if you are going to give them a bite to eat try and make it something very obviously home baked, or British. Nothing too fancy or sophisticated, and not a sit-down meal, because if all the family comes you're never going to have enough knives and forks to go round.

They all love fresh orange juice, and if you squeeze the oranges in advance you can keep them in the fridge until needed. Alan loves listening to music, especially Lennon and McCartney, so you might as well do the rounds of your friends and beg or borrow all their Beatles records. The Beatles records should go down well with Wayne, too, but in his case you would do well to add a Led Zeppelin album if you can. Wayne likes spicy food, sometimes Italian, so if you can make bread-type pastry, how about a really good jumbo-sized pizza to hand round in slabs?

I hope you like talking, for all the boys love a good conversation. Merrill and Mary are probably still full of ideas and enthusiasm about their house, so you'll be able to learn all about their home. If your father or brother are around they'll love swopping stories about decorating and do-it-yourself. Top of Merrill's list of priorities, after the house, is football. I hope they don't come to your home on a Saturday, because if they do, all the men will probably get glued to the afternoon sports programmes.

How about Jay? Well, his special favourite food is hamburgers, but don't be tempted to make English hamburgers for him, because there's a world of difference between the ones we have here and the sort they get in America. Jay is very fond of animals, and if you have a dog or a cat – or even a budgie – he'll be popular. He also likes telling jokes.

Donny loves to eat steaks and salads, but with the state of national economy the way it is at present he wouldn't be at all upset if you give the steak a miss and concentrated on producing a really good salad. Donny is also a bit of an electronic wizard, and he'll feel at home with your brother's train set.

You'll find you have a lot in common with sister Marie. She makes jewellery, and designs dresses, as well as collecting recipes. She has also studied shorthand and typing, which, she will tell you, is a great advantage to a girl.

And Jimmy? Well, Jimmy makes his own fun as he goes along, so he'll probably have all of you in stitches, and relaxed in no time.

And how about Mother and Father? Well, they like people to behave naturally, and to be straightforward. So they wouldn't be impressed if you broke the bank and tried to set up some fantastic party with expensive food or hired disco. So just be yourself, and you'll have a whale of a time.

Remember to have a good night's sleep beforehand, because they are all such live wires that you're going to be exhausted by the time you've finished entertaining them!

JIMMY

Just think of it. When Andy Williams first signed the singing Osmonds up all those years ago, Jimmy wasn't even born! It's hard to imagine the Osmond family without him, isn't it? He's a real character, as any of the family will tell you.

He began in showbiz at an even younger age than any of the others, when he was only three, while the family was touring Sweden, by performing *Red Roses for a Blue Lady*, and – wait for it – he sang it in Swedish, too. He couldn't actually read by then, so Mother and Father had to teach him the words phonetically. The audience went mad . . . they loved every minute of it, and Jimmy soon became a regular part of the act.

When the family went to Japan, Jimmy performed with the group, and this time sang a song in Japanese. As a result of this, Jimmy became very popular there, and soon had a hit record there, which stayed near the top for over four months. Jimmy was – as he sometimes reminds his brothers and sister – the first one to get to the top of the charts!

Jimmy's success abroad is probably due to the fact that he is such a good mimic. He can copy people so well that you'd never know it wasn't them – well, almost, anyway. He once did a take-off of Frank Sinatra singing *That's Life*, helped by Nancy Sinatra, when the family was appearing in Las Vegas. Frank saw the act and was very amused. He was so impressed that he later did an impression of Jimmy doing his impression!

Jimmy's first number one hit was *Long Haired Lover from Liverpool*, as you all know, and that was when he decided to introduce his footballer's high kick into his stage act!

He's very popular in his own family – and how many of us can say that about ourselves? He's always such a happy, uncomplicated person, that he gets on well with everyone. He's always willing to help, and he's always around when he's meant to be. He's a bit of a practical joker, too, and loves playing jokes on his brothers. For instance, he once told them that President Nixon had phoned and would call back later. I wonder how many members of the family expected the call to come!

He often teases his family, and thinks it's a great joke to get them to answer the door or the phone when no one's there at all. He loves food, too, more than anyone else. Once, he decided to open a restaurant at home, aided and abetted by Donny and Marie. He decided to put a lock on the fridge door and charge for food. The prices were inflationary, and very often the family had to buy food they hadn't even ordered. Very soon the food inspector, in the shape of Father Osmond, turned up and ordered the establishment to be closed on humanitarian grounds – otherwise half the family would run out of cash, and the other half were in danger of starving!

Jimmy is a great player of games. Here is a game which is very popular in Japan – where *he* is so popular, too. It's called Jumuku, and is a Japanese version of noughts and crosses. Two people can play together, and you need pencils and a piece of paper divided into twenty-one squares down and across. Player A marks crosses, and player B marks noughts, and they are drawn on the points where the lines cross. The idea of this game is to get five crosses or five noughts in a line in any direction. Another game you could play is to see who can draw the best picture of Mickey Mouse first. Don't play it with Jimmy, though – he's an expert at Mickey Mouse drawings and always wins!

There are a lot of people to whom the Osmonds are grateful, because they know that without them their lives would be quite, quite different.

The most important person to all the boys is YOU, their fan. In fact they like to think of each individual fan as a personal friend. There is nothing they like more than getting an opportunity to meet their fans, given half a chance. So every time they come over here, the Fan Club tries to arrange at least one informal face to face meeting with some of their fans.

As you probably know, the boys were given a chance to really prove themselves as entertainers on the Andy Williams show in the early 1960s. Andy showed great faith in them (there were only four singing in the group in those days, can you remember which ones?) and signed them up for a long term contract, which showed genius, don't you think.

One of the oldest friends of the Osmonds is Mike Curb, who signed the group up with MGM, and is the man responsible for Donny going solo, too. And Marie's first release was also Mike's idea. Mike has been a fantastic help to the group, leading them to greater heights with each recording.

Fish is another friend who has helped the group a great deal. He's called 'Fish' because Jay thought his name was Salmon. It isn't; it's Sammeth, Bill Sammeth, and he started with the Osmonds by handling publicity, and ended up doing the merchandising.

The group's management is organised by Ed Leffler, who works very hard. He arranges all the tours and shows, and has a very responsible job. He's the

one you need to get in touch with if you want the boys here more often!

Ed's assistant is Jim Morey. Not only does Jim have charge of the lighting for the shows, but is in charge of the travel arrangements. The group has never got lost yet, so you've got Jim to thank for that.

Masanobu Ono is one more person who looks after the boys. He knows where everything is, and keep all the equipment and costumes in working order.

Here in Britain there are some very special people whom the Osmonds work with.

First of all there is the lovely Maureen, who runs the Fan Club from London. Maureen, a busy mother with a family of her own to look after, is a second mother to the Osmonds when they come to Britain, and makes sure that they meet personally as many of the fans as possible.

Tony Prince, Tony Blackburn and Stewpot are all honorary members of the Osmonds Fan Club, and are always delighted to get Osmonds requests on their programmes. Tony Prince, in fact, is a friend of the family.

David Hughes, the Polydor recording representative, is another of their English friends. He is in constant touch with the family, and arranged all their British recordings, as well as fixing up press interviews, photographic sessions, and seeing to general public relations matters.

There are lots of other people to whom we should be grateful, helping and aiding the group both here and abroad, but out of all the people involved, we mustn't forget those wonderful people Mother and Father Osmond, without whom we wouldn't even have the boys!

UP, UP, A

Ever since Wayne was nine or ten years of age all he ever wanted for Christmas or birthdays were model aeroplanes. Then, when he was sixteen, he was delighted when Mother and Father gave him a course of lessons so that he could get his pilot's licence.

Because the family travels around so much, it would have been very difficult for Wayne to have attended actual lessons in aircraft instruction, so he had to learn a lot of the basic flying technique by correspondence. Then, when he could go no further without actually doing some flying himself, he was able to put his knowledge to good use when he continued his lessons, actually flying a plane with the help of an instructor. Then when he was eighteen, he was able to get his solo pilot's licence, which meant he became a fully qualified pilot.

When you lead the sort of full, exciting, jam-packed-with-action life of the Osmonds, you really appreciate the terrific sense of freedom which you feel when piloting an aeroplane through the blue, blue sky. It's like having a whole ocean all to yourself, says Wayne.

The aeroplane Wayne flies is a Cessna, which is very handy, especially for popping around in. More

ND AWAY

than once Wayne's knowledge of flying has saved the day when things have gone wrong.

Once, when the car broke down on the way to a filming engagement, they ended up by getting to the location in good time by finishing the journey in Wayne's plane.

Like all the Osmonds, Wayne is very talented. You usually see him playing rhythm guitar and saxophone on their shows on stage or television. But did you know that he also plays tenor banjo, the clarinet and the flute. Most of his spare time — when he's not working on their records and shows — is spent on his aeroplane, working on it and flying it.

But when he has a bit of extra free time, he likes to indulge his love of track events and archery. It's just as well that he's an active person, because he just loves Italian food — very fattening! And just think how fattening it could be if you indulged too often, and couldn't work it off.

Wayne says he likes girls. But most of all he likes girls who are 'real' people, and not at all phoney. He hates to meet people who put on an act when they see you, because acting and pretending to be someone you aren't is a sign of immaturity!

MARIE'S MART

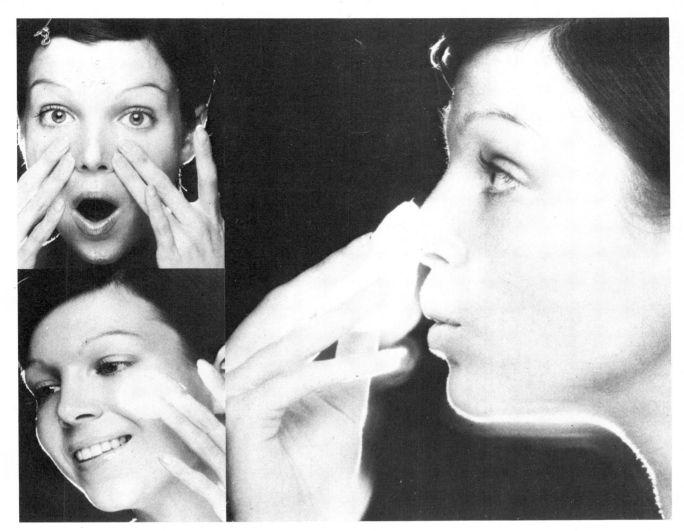

Marie Osmond has her own brand of organic cosmetics. Perhaps this is what helps her to look so fabulous all the time. She takes a lot of trouble and care with her make-up, and she said that before you even think of putting on make-up you must begin by thinking pretty. A healthy skin is a good foundation, and no amount of make-up will disguise bad skin, or unhealthy looking pores. Good skin begins in the kitchen – if you eat healthy, natural foods, then your skin and hair will be a lot better off than if you guzzle rubbish. She eats health-giving foods such as fresh fruit and juices, and lots of milk, and always tries to get fresh crisp vegetables. All of these help, you know, to make your complexion clear and glowing. Marie is lucky, as she has a good skin, with no problems.

But apart from a healthy diet, how about passing on a few of your tips, Marie?

"I like to experiment with all sorts of colours and tints," she told me. "Most boys, my brothers included, don't like a girl to be caked in make-up, but clever use of make-up can make a girl's face look thinner or fatter, change the shape of a nose, or tone down a heavy jawline. Make-up does work miracles for some people, doesn't it? It really is an eye opener to see well-known beauties before they put on their make-up – there's quite a noticeable difference!

"I put on my skin creams and lotions carefully, so that I never pull my face downwards. Pretend you're giving yourself an invisible face-lift, and always apply the cream in an upwards motion. First of all, I put a little cream or lotion in the palm of one hand, and pick it up with the fingertips of my other hand. I stroke it on to my face in an upwards motion, very gently. You may have noticed that most of my pictures show me smiling. Well, if you smile it shows a happy personality – and that's a skin treatment all by itself. I think that each time I smile I'm giving my face muscles a lift.

"When I apply a tonic, or freshener, I wet a pad of cotton wool in cool water, then after I've squeezed the water out I put some lotion on to the cotton wool. Then I pat my throat, and gently wipe and pat my neck and face. I take special care with the sections on my nose and chin which might get a bit oily. Some people hate freckles – need I say which ones? – think a sprinkling of freckles can be very attractive.

"When you are applying a base, put a little bit of foundation cream on your eyelids, because this prepares the eyes for eye make-up and gives it a good base. I think eye make-up is very important, as it's the first thing a boy sees when he looks at you.

"If you have a problem with a shiny nose, use a cream on your nose area to get rid of this shine. Then pat on an oil-absorbing powder.

"Sometimes when I'm at press conferences or on stage I find the lights get pretty hot, and this gives my make-up a shiny look. I usually press a paper tissue over my face, very gently, and then touch up my make-up with a cool powder, and maybe a little bit of colour. If my make-up gets that droopy look and I don't have time to re-do it, I sprinkle a few drops of freshener on a hanky, and go over my face, patting all over; then I pat it dry, and use powder to re-touch it.

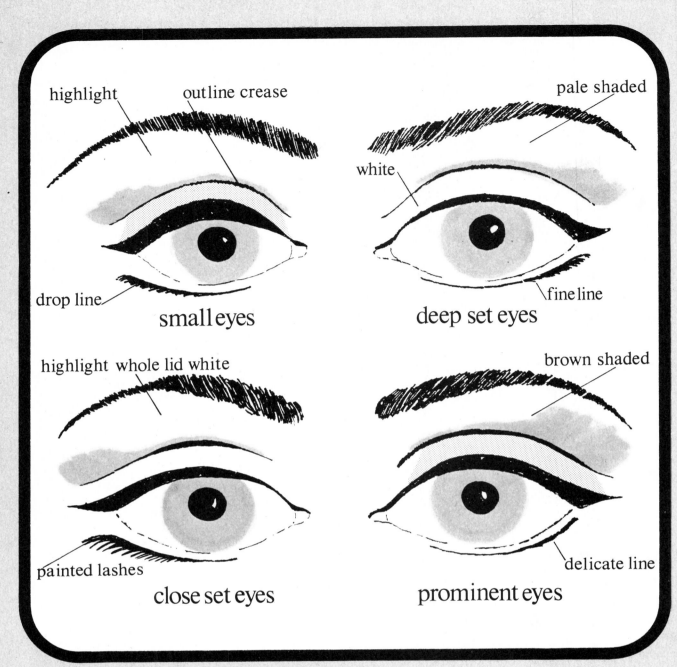

highlight   outline crease   pale shaded

white

drop line

fine line

small eyes   **deep set eyes**

highlight whole lid white   brown shaded

painted lashes

delicate line

close set eyes   **prominent eyes**

"Eye make-up is very, very important. And I spend a lot of time on my eyes. Your eyebrows and eye make-up should flatter you, and help to make your whole face pretty. If your face is oval, keep your eyebrows gently curved, and trim them carefully. You can wear almost any kind of look, but don't make your eyes look too round. With an oblong face you need fairly thick brows, and if you emphasise them with a pencil it helps to cut up the face so that it doesn't look quite so long.

"If you get dark shadows under your eyes 'cos you stayed up too late, or if you're feeling a bit off colour, you can disguise them by smoothing a pale shade of cream just over the dark patch. Mix it carefully, and then put on the rest of your make-up.

"I've found that the best way to put on eye liner is to paint it on. Stage lighting and other artificial light makes colour go flat, so I make up 'larger than life' when I'm going under the lights. I put a bit more colour on the lids; sometimes I even wear a touch of glittery shadow. I also accentuate my eyeline by painting on tiny 'lashes' at the outside of the lowest eyelid. Then I fill in these little 'lashes' with white shadow.

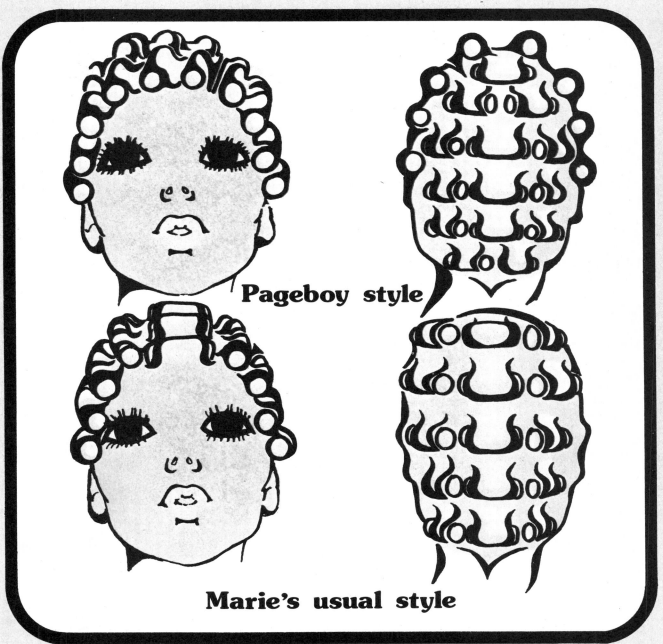

Pageboy style

Marie's usual style

"Another thing my brothers always notice, and that is a girl's hair. They like it to be nice and shining, and usually long-ish, if it suits the style of face. Not everyone can wear their hair long – some people look really gorgeous with short hair. I am very lucky because my hair is quite easy to look after, as it's long and heavy, with just a little bit of curl. When I set it up for very special occasions I use quite fat rollers, and just curl the hair in sections so that all the rollers are facing backwards. When it's dry I brush it well, and leave it as it falls – it looks more natural that way. Sometimes, just for a change, I give myself a pageboy, rolling it downwards all round, but with a side parting; at the very bottom row I use slightly smaller ones to encourage it to curl under."

GOIN' HOME

I'm a track star, gotta run far
And I'm ready to go.
It's a long, long road
And I gotta make it on my own.

Everybody's gaining on me
Tryin' to slow me down, but if
I'm gonna make it
Gotta fight, fight, fight all day
And night . . . and day . . . all right.

Chorus:
Goin' home, goin' home, goin' home,
I gotta make it, gonna make it all right
Goin' home, goin' home, goin' home,
If it takes me the rest of my life.

I'm a space man, from a different land
I gotta get back home.
I've been gone so long
That I'm feeling like a useless man.

Everybody's lookin' at me
Tryin' to help me down,
I gotta fight, fight, fight, even though it takes
Another day, and night, and day all right.

Oh my, why, why,
Is it either win or lose,
Somehow, someday,
I'll never ever have to go away.

Chorus:
Goin' home, goin' home, goin' home,
I gotta make it, gonna make it all right.
Goin' home, goin' home, goin' home,
I gotta make it, gonna make it all right.

© *Kolob Music USA*

AW and M Osmond

Answers

WELL, WHAT DO YOU KNOW?

How much did you know about the Osmonds, after all? Here are the answers to the questions on page 53.

1. *If Santa Were My Daddy*.
2. The Mormon Temple, Salt Lake City.
3. His bedroom.
4. Yes. They answer as many as they can.
5. Two.
6. Wayne and Jimmy.
7. He is the Osmonds' dog, and was adopted by a friend last year.
8. Chris, Lynn and, of course, Mary.
9. He is a Mormon Elder.
10. 4th May.
11. English. Their first language, because they are both deaf, is sign language.
12. Tommy is 26th October, and Virl is 19th October.
13. Bill Belew, who also makes Elvis Presley's costumes.
14. Jay.
15. Karate. The belt colour denotes the grade of expertise they each have reached.
16. *Paper Roses*, in 1973
17. Seven. Little did she know she'd have to add more!
18. They didn't. It just got learnt as they went along!
19. Root beer is made from roots and herbs, and natural flavourings. It is a natural drink which is very popular in America.
20. At McCormicks, in Chicago, when he was only four.